40 Weeks of Thoughts and Prayers

Pregnancy Devotional Journal

how do i feel? ____________

____

____

____

Week #: ______

- [ ] higher ♥ rate?
- [ ] emotional?
- [ ] warmer hands&feet?

- [ ] acne?
- [ ] increased thirst
- [ ] veins more notceable in breast?

Weight : ________

Waist Measurement : ______

Milestone : ____________

____

____

____

Cravings :

Things to pray for :

People to pray for :

Bible Verse for the day :

how do i feel? ______________

____

____

____

Week #: ______

- [ ] higher ♥ rate?
- [ ] emotional?
- [ ] warmer hands&feet?

- [ ] acne?
- [ ] increased thirst
- [ ] veins more noticeable in breast?

Weight : ________

Waist Measurement : ______

Milestone : ______________

____

____

____

Cravings :

Things to pray for :

People to pray for :

Bible Verse for the day :

how do i feel? ____________

____

____

____

Week #: ____

- [ ] higher ♥ rate?
- [ ] emotional?
- [ ] warmer hands&feet?

- [ ] acne?
- [ ] increased thirst
- [ ] veins more noticeable in breast?

Weight : ________

Waist Measurement : ______

Milestone : ____________

____

____

____

Cravings :

Things to pray for :

People to pray for :

Bible Verse for the day :

how do i feel? ____________

____

____

____

Week #: _____

- [ ] higher ♥ rate?
- [ ] emotional?
- [ ] warmer hands&feet?

- [ ] acne?
- [ ] increased thirst
- [ ] veins more noticeable in breast?

Weight : ________

Waist Measurement : ______

Milestone : ____________

____

____

____

Cravings :

Things to pray for :

People to pray for :

Bible Verse for the day :

how do i feel? ____________________

____

____

____

Week #: ______

- [ ] higher ♥ rate?
- [ ] emotional?
- [ ] warmer hands&feet?

- [ ] acne?
- [ ] increased thirst
- [ ] veins more noticeable in breast?

Weight : __________

Waist Measurement : _______

Milestone : ____________________

____

____

____

Cravings :

Things to pray for :

People to pray for :

Bible Verse for the day :

how do i feel? ______________

____

____

____

Week #: _____

- [ ] higher ♥ rate?
- [ ] emotional?
- [ ] warmer hands&feet?

- [ ] acne?
- [ ] increased thirst
- [ ] veins more noticeable in breast?

Weight : ________

Waist Measurement : ______

Milestone : ______________

____

____

____

Cravings :

Things to pray for :

People to pray for :

Bible Verse for the day :

Week #: _____

how do i feel? ____________

- [ ] higher ♥ rate?
- [ ] emotional?
- [ ] warmer hands&feet?

- [ ] acne?
- [ ] increased thirst
- [ ] veins more noticeable in breast?

Weight : ________

Waist Measurement : ______

Milestone : ____________

Cravings :

Things to pray for :

People to pray for :

Bible Verse for the day :

how do i feel? ____________

Week #: ____

- [ ] higher ♥ rate?
- [ ] emotional?
- [ ] warmer hands&feet?

- [ ] acne?
- [ ] increased thirst
- [ ] veins more noticeable in breast?

Weight : ________

Waist Measurement : ______

Milestone : ____________

Cravings :

Things to pray for :

People to pray for :

Bible Verse for the day :

how do i feel? ____________

____

____

____

Week #: ____

- [ ] higher ♥ rate?
- [ ] emotional?
- [ ] warmer hands&feet?

- [ ] acne?
- [ ] increased thirst
- [ ] veins more noticeable in breast?

Weight : ________

Waist Measurement : ______

Milestone : ____________

____

____

____

Cravings :

Things to pray for :

People to pray for :

Bible Verse for the day :

how do i feel? ______________

____

____

____

Week #: ______

- [ ] higher ♥ rate?
- [ ] emotional?
- [ ] warmer hands&feet?

- [ ] acne?
- [ ] increased thirst
- [ ] veins more noticeable in breast?

Weight : ________

Waist
Measurement : ______

Milestone : ______________

____

____

____

Cravings :

Things to pray for :

People to pray for :

Bible Verse for the day :

how do i feel? ____________

____

____

____

Week #: _____

- [ ] higher ♥ rate?
- [ ] emotional?
- [ ] warmer hands&feet?

- [ ] acne?
- [ ] increased thirst
- [ ] veins more noticeable in breast?

Weight : ________

Waist Measurement : ______

Milestone : ____________

____

____

____

Cravings :

Things to pray for :

People to pray for :

Bible Verse for the day :

how do i feel? ____________

____

____

____

Week #: ____

- [ ] higher ♥ rate?
- [ ] emotional?
- [ ] warmer hands&feet?

- [ ] acne?
- [ ] increased thirst
- [ ] veins more noticeable in breast?

Weight : ________

Waist Measurement : ______

Milestone : ____________

____

____

____

Cravings :

Things to pray for :

People to pray for :

Bible Verse for the day :

how do i feel? ______________

____

____

____

Week #: ______

- [ ] higher ♥ rate?
- [ ] emotional?
- [ ] warmer hands&feet?

- [ ] acne?
- [ ] increased thirst
- [ ] veins more noticeable in breast?

Weight : ________

Waist Measurement : ______

Milestone : ______________

____

____

____

Cravings :

Things to pray for :

People to pray for :

Bible Verse for the day :

how do i feel? ______________

____

____

____

Week #: _____

- [ ] higher ♥ rate?
- [ ] emotional?
- [ ] warmer hands&feet?

- [ ] acne?
- [ ] increased thirst
- [ ] veins more noticeable in breast?

Weight : ________

Waist Measurement : ______

Milestone : ______________

____

____

____

Cravings :

Things to pray for :

People to pray for :

Bible Verse for the day :

how do i feel? ____________

____

____

____

Week #: ____

- [ ] higher ♥ rate?
- [ ] emotional?
- [ ] warmer hands&feet?

- [ ] acne?
- [ ] increased thirst
- [ ] veins more noticeable in breast?

Weight : ________

Waist Measurement : ______

Milestone : ____________

____

____

____

Cravings :

Things to pray for :

People to pray for :

Bible Verse for the day :

how do i feel? ____________

Week #: _____

- [ ] higher ♥ rate?
- [ ] emotional?
- [ ] warmer hands&feet?

- [ ] acne?
- [ ] increased thirst
- [ ] veins more noticeable in breast?

Weight : ________

Waist Measurement : ______

Milestone : ____________

Cravings :

Things to pray for :

People to pray for :

Bible Verse for the day :

how do i feel? ____________

____

____

____

Week #: ____

- [ ] higher ♥ rate?
- [ ] emotional?
- [ ] warmer hands&feet?

- [ ] acne?
- [ ] increased thirst
- [ ] veins more noticeable in breast?

Weight : ________

Waist Measurement : ______

Milestone : ____________

____

____

____

Cravings :

Things to pray for :

People to pray for :

Bible Verse for the day :

how do i feel? ______________

____

____

____

Week #: _____

- [ ] higher ♥ rate?
- [ ] emotional?
- [ ] warmer hands&feet?

- [ ] acne?
- [ ] increased thirst
- [ ] veins more not ceable in breast?

Weight : ________

Waist Measurement : ______

Milestone : ______________

____

____

____

Cravings :

Things to pray for :

People to pray for :

Bible Verse for the day :

Week #: _____

how do i feel? ________________

____

____

____

- [ ] higher ♥ rate?
- [ ] emotional?
- [ ] warmer hands&feet?

- [ ] acne?
- [ ] increased thirst
- [ ] veins more noticeable in breast?

Weight : ________

Waist Measurement : ______

Milestone : ________________

____

____

____

Cravings :

Things to pray for :

People to pray for :

Bible Verse for the day :

how do i feel? ______

Week #: ____

- [ ] higher ❤ rate?
- [ ] emotional?
- [ ] warmer hands&feet?

- [ ] acne?
- [ ] increased thirst
- [ ] veins more noticeable in breast?

Weight : ______

Waist Measurement : ______

Milestone : ______

Cravings :

Things to pray for :

People to pray for :

Bible Verse for the day :

how do i feel? ____________

____
____
____

Week #: ______

- [ ] higher ♥ rate?
- [ ] emotional?
- [ ] warmer hands&feet?

- [ ] acne?
- [ ] increased thirst
- [ ] veins more noticeable in breast?

Weight : ________

Waist Measurement : ______

Milestone : ____________

____
____
____

Cravings :

Things to pray for :

People to pray t~for :

Bible Verse for the day :

how do i feel? ____________

____

____

____

Week #: ____

- [ ] higher ♥ rate?
- [ ] emotional?
- [ ] warmer hands&feet?

- [ ] acne?
- [ ] increased thirst
- [ ] veins more noticeable in breast?

Weight : ________

Waist Measurement : ______

Milestone : ____________

____

____

____

Cravings :

Things to pray for :

People to pray for :

Bible Verse for the day :

how do i feel? ______________

____

____

____

Week #: _____

- [ ] higher ♥ rate?
- [ ] emotional?
- [ ] warmer hands&feet?

- [ ] acne?
- [ ] increased thirst
- [ ] veins more noticeable in breast?

Weight : ________

Waist Measurement : ______

Milestone : ______________

____

____

____

Cravings :

Things to pray for :

People to pray for :

Bible Verse for the day :

how do i feel? ______

______
______
______

Week #: ____

- [ ] higher ♥ rate?
- [ ] emotional?
- [ ] warmer hands&feet?

- [ ] acne?
- [ ] increased thirst
- [ ] veins more noticeable in breast?

Weight : ______

Waist
Measurement : ______

Milestone : ______

______
______
______

Cravings :

Things to pray for :

People to pray for :

Bible Verse for the day :

how do i feel? ______________

____

____

____

Week #: _____

- [ ] higher ♥ rate?
- [ ] emotional?
- [ ] warmer hands&feet?

- [ ] acne?
- [ ] increased thirst
- [ ] veins more noticeable in breast?

Weight : ________

Waist Measurement : ______

Milestone : ______________

____

____

____

Cravings :

Things to pray for :

People to pray for :

Bible Verse for the day :

how do i feel? ______________

____

____

____

Week #: _____

- [ ] higher ♥ rate?
- [ ] emotional?
- [ ] warmer hands&feet?

- [ ] acne?
- [ ] increased thirst
- [ ] veins more noticeable in breast?

Weight : ________

Waist Measurement : ______

Milestone : ______________

____

____

____

Cravings :

Things to pray for :

People to pray for :

Bible Verse for the day :

how do i feel? ______________

____

____

____

Week #: _____

- [ ] higher ♥ rate?
- [ ] emotional?
- [ ] warmer hands&feet?

- [ ] acne?
- [ ] increased thirst
- [ ] veins more noticeable in breast?

Weight : ________

Waist Measurement : ______

Milestone : ______________

____

____

____

Cravings :

Things to pray for :

People to pray for :

Bible Verse for the day :

how do i feel? ______________

____

____

____

Week #: _____

- [ ] higher ♥ rate?
- [ ] emotional?
- [ ] warmer hands&feet?

- [ ] acne?
- [ ] increased thirst
- [ ] veins more noticeable in breast?

Weight : ________

Waist Measurement : ______

Milestone : ______________

____

____

____

Cravings :

Things to pray for :

People to pray for :

Bible Verse for the day :

how do i feel? ____________

____

____

____

Week #: _____

- [ ] higher ♥ rate?
- [ ] emotional?
- [ ] warmer hands&feet?

- [ ] acne?
- [ ] increased thirst
- [ ] veins more noticeable in breast?

Weight : ________

Waist Measurement : ______

Milestone : ____________

____

____

____

Cravings :

Things to pray for :

People to pray for :

Bible Verse for the day :

how do i feel? ______________

____

____

____

Week #: _____

- [ ] higher ♥ rate?
- [ ] emotional?
- [ ] warmer hands&feet?

- [ ] acne?
- [ ] increased thirst
- [ ] veins more noticeable in breast?

Weight : ________

Waist Measurement : ______

Milestone : ______________

____

____

____

Cravings :

Things to pray for :

People to pray for :

Bible Verse for the day :

how do i feel? ______________

____

____

____

Week #: ____

- [ ] higher ♥ rate?
- [ ] emotional?
- [ ] warmer hands&feet?

- [ ] acne?
- [ ] increased thirst
- [ ] veins more noticeable in breast?

Weight : ________

Waist Measurement : ______

Milestone : ______________

____

____

____

Cravings :

Things to pray for :

People to pray for :

Bible Verse for the day :

how do i feel? ____________

____

____

____

Week #: _____

- [ ] higher ♥ rate?
- [ ] emotional?
- [ ] warmer hands&feet?

- [ ] acne?
- [ ] increased thirst
- [ ] veins more noticeable in breast?

Weight : ________

Waist Measurement : ______

Milestone : ______________

____

____

____

Cravings :

Things to pray for :

People to pray for :

Bible Verse for the day :

how do i feel? ______________

____

____

____

Week #: ____

- [ ] higher ♥ rate?
- [ ] emotional?
- [ ] warmer hands&feet?

- [ ] acne?
- [ ] increased thirst
- [ ] veins more noticeable in breast?

Weight : ________

Waist Measurement : ______

Milestone : ______________

____

____

____

Cravings :

Things to pray for :

People to pray for :

Bible Verse for the day :

how do i feel? ______________________

____

____

____

Week #: ______

- [ ] higher ♥ rate?
- [ ] emotional?
- [ ] warmer hands&feet?

- [ ] acne?
- [ ] increased thirst
- [ ] veins more noticeable in breast?

Weight : __________

Waist Measurement : ______

Milestone : ______________________

____

____

____

Cravings :

Things to pray for :

People to pray for :

Bible Verse for the day :

Week #: ____

how do i feel? ____________

____

____

____

- [ ] higher ♥ rate?
- [ ] emotional?
- [ ] warmer hands&feet?

- [ ] acne?
- [ ] increased thirst
- [ ] veins more noticeable in breast?

Weight : ________

Waist Measurement : ______

Milestone : ____________

____

____

____

Cravings :

Things to pray for :

People to pray for :

Bible Verse for the day :

how do i feel? ______________

____

____

____

Week #: _____

- [ ] higher ♥ rate?
- [ ] emotional?
- [ ] warmer hands&feet?

- [ ] acne?
- [ ] increased thirst
- [ ] veins more noticeable in breast?

Weight : ________

Waist Measurement : ______

Milestone : ______________

____

____

____

Cravings :

Things to pray for :

People to pray for :

Bible Verse for the day :

how do i feel? ____________

____

____

____

Week #: _____

- [ ] higher ♥ rate?
- [ ] emotional?
- [ ] warmer hands&feet?

- [ ] acne?
- [ ] increased thirst
- [ ] veins more noticeable in breast?

Weight : ________

Waist Measurement : ______

Milestone : ____________

____

____

____

Cravings :

Things to pray for :

People to pray for :

Bible Verse for the day :

how do i feel? ______________

____

____

____

Week #: _____

- [ ] higher ♥ rate?
- [ ] emotional?
- [ ] warmer hands&feet?

- [ ] acne?
- [ ] increased thirst
- [ ] veins more noticeable in breast?

Weight : ________

Waist Measurement : ______

Milestone : ______________

____

____

____

Cravings :

Things to pray for :

People to pray for :

Bible Verse for the day :

how do i feel? ______________

____

____

____

Week #: _____

- [ ] higher ♥ rate?
- [ ] emotional?
- [ ] warmer hands&feet?

- [ ] acne?
- [ ] increased thirst
- [ ] veins more noticeable in breast?

Weight : ________

Waist Measurement : ______

Milestone : ______________

____

____

____

Cravings :

Things to pray for :

People to pray for :

Bible Verse for the day :

how do i feel? ______________

____

____

____

Week #: _____

- [ ] higher ♥ rate?
- [ ] emotional?
- [ ] warmer hands&feet?

- [ ] acne?
- [ ] increased thirst
- [ ] veins more noticeable in breast?

Weight : ________

Waist Measurement : ______

Milestone : ______________

____

____

____

Cravings :

Things to pray for :

People to pray for :

Bible Verse for the day :

www.ingramcontent.com/pod-product-compliance
Lightning Source LLC
LaVergne TN
LVHW080848170826
845678LV00006B/1747

9798869444400